south

in

the

world

About the Author

Lisa Jacobson is an award-winning poet and fiction writer. Her verse novel *The Sunlit Zone* (Five Islands Press, 2012) won the 2014 Adelaide Festival Awards John Bray Poetry Prize. This book was shortlisted for four other national awards, including the Prime Minister's Literary Awards and the inaugural Stella Prize for Australian women's writing. An earlier poetry collection, *Hair & Skin & Teeth* (Five Islands Press, 1995), was shortlisted for the National Book Council Awards. In 2011 she won the Bruce Dawe National Poetry Prize. Her work has been published in Australia, Canada, Indonesia, the United Kingdom and the United States. She studied literature at Melbourne and La Trobe Universities, and remains an Honorary Research Fellow at La Trobe. She lives in Melbourne with her partner and daughter. www.lisajacobson.org

Praise for *THE SUNLIT ZONE*

If poetry has lost its way in the world, been relegated by the current generation to an earlier sensibility no longer suited to the fast-paced, quick-fix, electronic world of the twenty-first century, this is the book to lead it back. *The Sunlit Zone* is a success in many genres – speculative fiction, memoir, fiction – and most brilliantly as finely-crafted, highly-imaginative poetry. As a verse novel set in 2050, it foretells skinfones, UV quotas, nappy plugs and fruit salad trees, but it's set against the universal, for-all-ages, backdrop of birth, love and death. The theme of disability is handled with gentle respect as are the many threads running through this intriguing story. This verse novel is memorable and inspirational.
WINNER, 2014 ADELAIDE FESTIVAL AWARDS, JOHN BRAY POETRY PRIZE

In *The Sunlit Zone,* Lisa Jacobson has produced an altogether remarkable piece of work. Few narrative poems from this country can even compare with it. Flowing and emotionally subtle, it nevertheless encompasses both science fiction and the colours of fantasy. The generational stories of a family are mingled with something of Ovid's *Metamorphosis,* yet the story somehow flows with ease. Moreover, the little world of our seaside surf townships is vividly evoked both in its present form and in some bold, imagined future. It remains utterly readable, for all its strangeness.
SHORTLISTED, 2013 PRIME MINISTER'S LITERARY AWARDS

Set in the near future with a narrative arc spanning 30 years from 2020 to 2050, *The Sunlit Zone* is by turns playfully ethereal and darkly disturbing, not least for the unsettling familiarity of the damaged world it presents as our possible future. Only after one has plumbed the depths and stared into the abyss can one fully appreciate the dazzling riches of a place that teems with life, though not necessarily life as we know it.
LIAM DAVISON, *THE AUSTRALIAN*

Praise for *THE SUNLIT ZONE* (continued)

This original and surprising book combines two genres rarely seen out together: speculative fiction and the verse novel. Set on the east coast of Australia between 2020 and 2050, the novel uses recognisable settings and familiar characters to represent a world in which technology may change the daily texture of human life but human character doesn't change much at all. Jacobson imagines a world that is radically different from ours in some ways but in others disconcertingly the same; love stories and family tragedies alike have the same qualities as the ones we all know, as do the experiences of loss and recovery.
SHORTLISTED, 2013 STELLA PRIZE

Much of the addictive quality comes from the sheer skill with which Jacobson builds narrative suspense and unfolds character and cultural situation, in an ecocidally blighted Melbourne around 2050.
SHORTLISTED, 2012 WESLEY MICHEL WRIGHT POETRY PRIZE

The Sunlit Zone is a moving elegy of love and loss presented in the form of a speculative verse novel. The judges admired its narrative sweep and the compelling family dynamic that drives it. The novel transports the reader to a haunted future, minting new words for a new world while remaining firmly connected to the familiar. It is a risk-taking work of rare, imaginative power.
SHORTLISTED, 2009 VICTORIAN PREMIER'S LITERARY AWARD
FOR AN UNPUBLISHED MANUSCRIPT

south in the world

lisa jacobson

UWA PUBLISHING

First published in 2014 by
UWA Publishing
Crawley, Western Australia 6009
www.uwap.uwa.edu.au

UWAP is an imprint of UWA Publishing
a division of The University of Western Australia

This book is copyright. Apart from any fair dealing for the purpose of private study,
research, criticism or review, as permitted under the *Copyright Act 1968*,
no part may be reproduced by any process without written permission.
Enquiries should be made to the publisher.

Copyright © Lisa Jacobson 2014

The moral right of the author has been asserted.

National Library of Australia
Cataloguing-in-Publication entry:

Jacobson, Lisa, author.
South in the world / Lisa Jacobson.
ISBN: 9781742586021 (paperback)
Australian poetry.
A821.3

Typeset in Bembo by Lasertype
Printed by Lightning Source
Cover photograph by Mike Raker
Author photograph by Hayley Austen

This project has been assisted by the Australian Government
through the Australia Council, its arts funding and advisory body.

For Hayley

Contents

Part 1

Several Ways to Fall Out of the Sky	3
Emergence	5
The Memory Wire	6
Stable Boys	7
On Teaching My Daughter to Ride a Horse	9
Why, When We Fall Off Things, We Fall Down	10
Take-Off	11
The Traffic of Angels	13
Signs of Life	14
Sadness	15
Wheelbarrow	16
Longevity	17
The Stepfather Project	18
Kairos, or The Right Time	19
Habits Formed by Eternity	22

Part 2

Girls and Horses in the Fire	25
South in the World: Thinking about Black Saturday from the Swiss Alps	26
This Newfound Note	30
Releasing the Frog	31
Trout Farm	32
Limping into Jerusalem	33
Photographs of Jews	34

Anne Frank's Sister Falls from Her Bunk	36
Old Nazis	37
Why Old People Talk about Their Operations	38
The Concept of Necessity in Marx and Angels	39
Thylacine	41
Calling Up the Dead	42
Some Adjustments to the Original Idea	45

Part 3

All Things	49
Night Feeding	50
The Virgin Mary Gets Postnatal Depression	51
Ellipsis	54
Amphibian	55
Tall Ships	56
Silver City	57
The God You Don't Believe In	58
Those for Whom the Metaphors Are Invented	61
In My Mother's Kitchen	62
Orbit	63
Exodus	64
Walking the Black Dog	65
Vanishing Point	69

Part 4

The Way We Do In Sex	73
Triage	74
Morning Ride	75
Who Is To Say	76
Holiday Season	77

Thoughts between Christmas and New Year 78
   (i) Forgetting to buy the nets 78
   (ii) Material in excess of 2 cubic metres 79
   (iii) But then, that said 80
Moorings 81
What to Expect 82
Waking from Hibernation 83
First Cigarette 84
Dragonfly 85

Part 5

There Are Stones That Sing 89
Shift Work 90
   (i) Case Notes 90
   (ii) Wild Rabbits 91
   (iii) Talking about Country 92
   (iv) Incident Report 93
Dutch Tulip Bubble 94
Spinning on a Dream Thread 95
Open Plan Office 96
Virga, or No Rain Falling 97
The Leaf Sweeper 98
War Horse 100
Another Poem about Dogs 101
Small Deaths 102
The Interior Ladder 103

A note on the text 107
Sources for the epigraphs 107
Author's note 109

– 1 –

Several Ways to Fall Out of the Sky

Forget to take your wings from where they hang in the hall, the brass hook silent as a question mark beneath silver feathers.

Remember to collect your wings, having noticed the post-it note on the bench that says 'wings'. But in your haste to take flight, forget to fasten their buckles.

Become mesmerised by the sun, bigger now than the world below. Forget to flap.

Ignore any doubts about low-flying above a somnolent bay where a ploughman works doggedly on in furrows of soil, and Daedalus calls out your name.

Lose faith in the universe, the laws of physics, the invention of flight.

Forget to breathe.

Consider the way gravity swings the planets round, pulls tides up shores, draws blood from women.

Discover profiles of loved ones in the clouds – your mother with her back half-turned, your daughter dissolving as you wing towards her.

Remember unwashed clothes, wisdom not yet taught to kids, pets gone hungry, the goldfish, the goldfish…

Be totally unable to remember the author of *The Grapes of Wrath*; only that the Japanese translation was *The Angry Raisins*.

Find remorse weighing heavier on your shoulders than wings.

Fly into the flight path of pelicans that peck at your hair for their nests – which throws you right out.

Crash into Mt Sugarloaf, graceless as a kettle crash-landing the moon.

Seek out the floor of heaven, the face of God.

Soar too high in winter. Feel ice freeze your wings over, as it does all other high-fliers: winged horses, ghost ships, over-ambitious angels.

Fall asleep in the air. Remember this: no one knows who you are.

Emergence

From this distance, I'm small and quiet,
being all curled up in this poem and waiting

inside the woman who lies spread-eagled,
silenced by the temperament of generations.

My father cradles a book, whose contents
no one remembers, and as he reads

she listens, not to this, but to the sharp unfurl of wings
within our dim-lit cave; her muscular breath.

Slow march of words crawling back through centuries,
letters inked into leather scrolls,

a dark wind lifting the skin of memory
and my mother labouring me to the world's fleshy rim

beyond which lie the nameless continents
of milk, breath, hope, time, sleep.

The Memory Wire

When I was twelve and in love with horses,
my best friend's dad sold fencing wire.
Circling the building where he worked
was a moat of paddock hemmed by fence
where my friend's bay mare grazed;
sleek, long and lean, both girl and horse,
and hard to say which was more beautiful.

Then I knew, the way horses do,
when they crash their hard bulk about,
that there'd be theft, and damage done.
Often a strange sorrow filled my hours.
This was in the days of childhood
yet I was happy then.

Stable Boys

A barn dance at the stables
on Christmas Eve, the fence posts
strung with tinsel, the ménage

lit up with coloured lights.
I let myself be led, that summer night,
by the brother of a friend

who kept her horses here with mine,
away from the dancing, swaying crowd
to a beat-up Ford sedan.

Boys passed a bourbon bottle around
but I sat quiet on the car's back seat
with vinyl clinging to my legs,

not knowing quite what to do or say
until I heard the click of car doors lock
and some boy's hand snake up my dress

and down between my thighs.
The handle, when I tugged,
refused to yield,

so I said, 'Let me out!' Kicking
the front seat hard with riding boots
until one of them relented.

'C'mon, mate, just let her go,' he said.
The other withdrew his serpent arm.
'Mate, c'mon, fucken let her go!'

And they did then.
I half fell from the car
and ran away through darkness.

On Teaching My Daughter to Ride a Horse

Up on the horse,
she is another kind of creature;
equine and winged,
this fire-lit child who says:
'Trot, mama, trot!' and,
'Are we galloping yet?'
Her legs clamp around the horse's girth
the way they used to clamp to me
when I'd support her on my hip
or stoop to put her down
(too heavy for that now).
Her squealing trill like a horse's laugh,
a kicking up of the heels,
meadow-grass sound that proves
whoever invented daughters
and horses knows their grace;
the way both toss their manes to the wind,
their velvet (no other word for it)
pelt and skin, their sweet hay-breath,
and a lot of other things.

Why, When We Fall Off Things, We Fall Down

Cycling together on the path
that threads through river grass,

swallows paddling the bluest sky,
my daughter asks me why,

when we fall off things, we fall down.
So I tell her about gravity

and how the spinning world pulls us
towards its girth and holds us close,

and how without it we'd go soaring
into the mouths of distant galaxies.

She looks up then into the sky
beyond boat-shaped clouds

until we reach a steep incline
and the bike's slowed revolutions

demand her full attention
as we pedal up the hill.

Take-Off

I am dreaming of you nightly now,
galloping white and luminous
against the sky

and closer than ever before.
Your coiled and well-hinged wings
seem too corporeal to keep us up.

Yet you are flying.
Great hooves crash
through the tops of trees

at the edge of all possible forests.
Steering us on through mute
and feathery darkness.

The world rolls below,
softened by cloud
and uncomplicated

until we land upon it.
One final toss of your mane
and you scatter like salt.

At breakfast I compare you
with other wonders real and imagined:
cities sinking on crusty haunches,

gold towers scraping the painted heavens,
red horses poised on the dreamy edge
of light and invention.

Today I go out to the stables
where the hay smells sweet as wine,
run my hands along the grey mare's spine

and feel the swell of wings
beneath her skin.
It will not be long before take-off.

The Traffic of Angels
After *Jacob's Ladder* by William Blake

The angels' tread upon the stairs leaves no imprint.
Lightly they move, escorting the dazed
and newly dead before climbing down
    to earth again.

And all its heaviness they elect to greet
as readily as the gold and airy thinness
of those upper rungs, still marked and bent
by Lucifer's fall.
    There is peril when angels descend.
Do their wings ice over?
Are they touched by our brute calamity?

We don't hear them breathe,
although perhaps that's what they do
as soon as they touch down.
    Is the air harsh in their throats?
Does it constrict and barb
these creatures so unused to air?
The dead weight of oxygen;
its brash insistence.

Signs of Life

Despite my broody vigilance,
not all the eggs hold life.
And yet, what wonder in the darkness!
The bell curve of my torch reveals
three embryos tucked in shells,
whose shifts and turns recall to me
the miracle of your quickening.

So now I'm on the phone to you,
with one runt chick new-hatched
and cheeping in my hand,
while you tell me between sobs
that nothing's wrong
— except you miss me, this late hour,
in your father's house.
I press the phone against my ear
until your sobs subside,
and you fall back
into the feather-warmth of sleep.

Sadness

Last night I sat in our new flat
on an unpacked box of clothes and howled

while my daughter, her own crying ceased,
stood before me, damp and pink from the bath,

and remembering what makes me laugh,
slid her fists into the sleeves of her red jumper

that some aunt or other had knitted, the seams
already unravelling, and said, church-quiet,

'Look Mum, where are my hands?'
I laughed then and held her close,

saying, 'The sadness is gone a bit now. It's going now.'
And by morning it had, flapping away on sullen wings

back to the place where all sad things go, over the hill,
just there, where the cockatoos shriek out

a raucous symphony, beyond the river of trees
and further still. 'See?' I say, pointing. 'See?'

Wheelbarrow

1.
In the beginning there was the wheelbarrow, which they kept in the bedroom and filled with books, fruit and phone messages.

2.
Later when the sleeplessness got too much, they used it to wheel each other around the house. Once they filled it with soup, which they ladled into bowls and ate with chunks of bread.

3.
The wheelbarrow was silver. It glittered in the dark and made whistling sounds like birdsong. Sometimes it hummed.

4.
Once, she pushed him backwards into the wheelbarrow and tossed the book after him, saying, 'Stay there until you've read the first act of *Hamlet* at least!'

5.
It was a little awkward making love in the wheelbarrow. Its base was cold against their flanks. But they persisted, and over time became so used to it they felt odd making love anywhere else.

6.
Most wheelbarrows have an innate understanding of love.

Longevity

There are ghosts of me here,
and a trace of the old circle
in the grass my father mowed
so we girls could ride our horses
in the park. We reach the metal
gate that leads up to the paddock
and beyond, the house where I
lived when young.

'I often pause my walking
here to take a rest,' you say.
'This road, this house.'
I called out once at this very gate
to a god I wasn't sure was there.
And thirty years later here you are:
the odd longevity of prayer.

The Stepfather Project

You and my daughter have been working
on a delicate long-term project, of sorts.

Some kind of garment, made from false starts,
sourced from the fifth chamber in your heart.

'Too much big words,' she used to say,
this jealous girl-shaped gangster child.

But now she's found there's much to like
in your gruff, broad-shouldered scholarly style.

You read Yeats and German philosophy.
She's into YouTube and *Modern Family*.

But you've worked the wheel till something's
formed, seven years in the making

and unfinished of course, but even so,
offering shelter and warmth.

Kairos, or The Right Time
Alice Springs, 2013

(i)
This desert town still holds you in its thrall,
although the house your father bought is gone
and all your straggly mates.

Who knows what has become of them?
The clouds of budgerigars are as shrill
as ever, though more scarce.

The rocks recline where they always
did, colossal as memory, the trees
that flank the Todd still sink their roots

into the water table beneath the dried-up
river bed, where the Arrernte men
sleep off their social security cheques

or make the slow trek into town for grog
and bread, or sit out the noonday heat
on blankets with their wives and kids.

(ii)
That sudden exodus to Alice Springs
left no time for sentiment;
your pigeons clueless in their aviary.

You thought it was a holiday, too young
to comprehend your sister's ragged breath
as spurs that had your parents fleeing

Melbourne's soupy air towards the only place
the doctors said could save her now.
The desert town a salve that sang her back

into herself and drained the swamp inside
her lungs. The Preston house was sold;
somehow your parents found new jobs.

So much red space and blue sky
after the green canopies of home;
the caterpillar ridges of Yipirinya.

(iii)
So now your sister's dead,
after the madness that besieged
those later years, her fractured

paranoia and her unkempt hair.
News of her sudden death falls
hard on you in wintry Melbourne,

where you finally made your home.
For Alice never had that much to offer
boys back then, once they were grown.

And yet those underwater tables still
run deep and feed the roots of your wild
imaginings. For that was where the child

was trowelled into a man; in the red dirt
upheaval made to save your sister's life,
which ended up by saving yours instead.

Habits Formed by Eternity

God falls to earth with a resounding clang
and wonders what he's up against,
the insects like meteors to his sensitive ears.
God has big ears, celestially dinted,
and feet rough as afterthoughts. He moves
them carefully, trying not to break things.

Dog-tired, God is, in his faded cardigan,
wishing we'd made him more stylish
or different somehow. He flares vast nostrils,
the same that parted oceans and let Moses through.
Beyond he smells seagulls, war and felony,
the galaxy, old gods, space junk.

The bush is shrill with heat and atrocity.
Blowflies hover like small black angels
and nothing looks finished, not even creation.
When he opens his book, ants track fiercely
across the print; red bull ants with well-made joints.
He flicks them off unthinkingly.

God reads slowly, a habit formed by eternity.
New stars are discovered and cures for cancer
but not much else. A woman turns like fruit
to the light. God hears her heart beat:
kaboom! kaboom! and travels towards it,
to sit with her loneliness up against his.

– 2 –

Girls and Horses in the Fire
Kinglake, Black Saturday 2009

Nothing will come between them,
those girls and their horses;
not wind or rain, nor pillars of fire.
If a hand should flick a match
amongst leaves, or trunks implode
with the weight of heat, or lightning
blast the wasted trees, still they'd run,
these girls, through conflagrations,
wreathed by flames and embers.
Girls who run towards horses in fire,
may you find your home in the equine stars:
Pegasus, Equuleus. Hush, sleep now.

South in the World
Thinking about Black Saturday from the Swiss Alps

1.
The charcoal forest is greening.
Bright leaves unfold from trunks
wherever they can, stampeding
for light and air. Yet some trees
remain black and dead. Nothing
grows on them or ever will.
The people are the same,
unfurling from the stumps of hearts
or falling backwards into them.
Called or not called, the fire god
soars, uttering its newborn caw,
resounding with fierce resilience.

2.
I write this from a distant city
of slender, fine-spun churches
and trains that run on time,
the air distilled by alpine snow.
In Fraumünster Cathedral,
Chagall's *Green Christ* drifts up
through arcs of painted glass,
backlit by temperate sunlight.
The spirit takes flight as nails
sink into skin, the cross dissolves
into leaves, becomes a ring,
a hoop of gold rising above
tree-level.

3.
South in the world, everyone
is weeping. A litany of loss rouses
earlier griefs that once lay sleeping.
This first winter makes living cold.
Men hunker down in tents and vans,
make fires in kero cans for warmth.
The town is still hoarse with talk.
'Fire, fire, fire,' the people mutter
in the temporary village and shops,
in the pub and makeshift post office,
until the word is emptied of meaning.

4.
In Sils Maria, where Anne Frank
spent two summers and Nietzsche
found clarity in the rarefied air,
resurrection is everywhere
greening the hills. Snowmelt
rushes down mountains to greet
the meadows in flurries of joy,
wildflowers sprinkle fields.
It's hard to think of fire here
in this land of clocks and cowbells
where nature is not at war;
even the avalanches fall softly,
with a gentle roar.

5.
You who saw the firestorm's rage
and somehow managed to escape
the flames that took whole families
and (must we say it?) children,
babies. I could list them forever:
the petrified horses, the dazed wombats,
the kangaroos in an incendiary pack.
Did the Green Christ see them
and who can answer all of this?
Whom then can we blame?

6.
The alps rear high above the lake.
I wake to see their whiteness
satiate the windows in this room
with a diamantine ferocity,
so vast the mind suspects illusion.
In midwinter this cold can kill:
cattle cram the rough-hewn barns.
But with edelweiss clambering
over beams and thatch, it's hard
to imagine the force of it.

7.
Angels were of no help that day,
flying in on burning wings
and crashing to the ground.
Few who found the ragged heaps
saw the mark of their divinity.
Some took them home to bury
in their burnt-out yards.
But angels are no match for fireballs,
their garments a trap for embers.
And anyway, didn't we lose our need
for angels long before these fires?
For whoever has seen them,
few believe.

8.
Those of you who returned to see
the things no one should ever see,
corpses in cars and prone in baths;
you whose names are listed and filed
in the databases of council shires
as survivors of those deceased by fire;
you who endured that unendurable night,
praying that the dead were still alive:
is it too much to grasp the greening of things
that were black and charred?
The body burnt and pierced floats
ever skyward. Keep your eyes on it.

This Newfound Note

Something flew in my window last night
when I let the rain-washed autumn in,
and this morning found it trembling
in the corner of my kitchen sink;
a diurnal insect that oddly trekked
the dark where moths and quiet owls sit.
My thumb and finger clamp the wings
that struggle with a sudden strength,
the legs clawing like small bent pins
as I carry it to the windowsill.
Small-time lepidopterist for a minute,
with chloroform nudging at my hip
and a glass case neat with specimens,
pretty as gems and opalescent.
I loosen my grip and off it flits,
irregular as a newfound note
that gradually resumes musicality.
I can well imagine it, this life unlived.

Releasing the Frog

Sitting beside my letterbox,
a large and elderly frog,
slack-bellied and scarce a pulse
beneath its double chin.
Even so I scoop it up.
Life stirs its porous skin.
River weeds trail weepily,
the banks softened by rain
that fell last week so heavily
the very sky collapsed
beneath its weight.
When I am dying, carry me
down to this same river.
Let the water do its work.
Let time shuck off my human form
and return me to the fish-scaled thing
that I once was; begin.

Trout Farm

That day we caught the trout:
I reeled it in, all silvery and gasping,
my husband removed the hook,
then slammed down hard on its head
with a chunk of wood. Three times
he struck before the fish lay quiet.
Soon there'd be trout with butter, frying,
and we grew hungry just thinking about it.
But a few days passed, and several more,
and still we didn't eat it; lying stiff in ice
at the back of the freezer, with its eyes
wide open, so I couldn't tell if it died
in shock, or not.

Limping into Jerusalem
New Imperial Hotel, Old City

Limping on my sprained and swollen ankle
through the Jaffa Gate in homage to my tribe:
'Be healed,' said the stones, trembling in the walls.
'Be healed,' cried the path King David trod.

Who else once trawled these limestone streets
for talismans or clutched at Christ's own robes,
hoping to be healed of leprosy or blindness?

Those ancient kin who built Jerusalem
had been less than a memory until now,
my diaspora so well-worn, it scarcely
chafed at all.

The Arab who carried my suitcase
didn't steal it, as my father said he would,
as I limped into the nearest hotel;
imperial, peeling, faded.

'Ice, *oy vey*!' said the landlady.
'Prayer,' said a nun in an upright chair.
'Boiling water,' said the Arab.

All day I watched the confluence of faiths
collide and merge like rivers beneath
my balcony.

Hassidic Jews in long black coats
strode briskly through the twilight.
My foot grew strong. Blue stars
on white flags, bringing me home.

Photographs of Jews
Yad Vashem, Jerusalem

1) An orphan child
crawling in the ghetto
like a dog.

2) A woman, wild-eyed as a deer,
staring at the muzzle of a camera.

3) A father pointing to the sky
to ensure his son sees this
and not the brink of a muddy pit
where corpses lie in a casual heap.
The guards have raised their guns.
Birds wheel above, unimpeded.

I have dreamt of rough serge coats,
of escaping camps
and being sent to them,
of hiding in groves of trees.

I am a Dachau Jew with a yellow star
staring down the barrel of that camera.
I am digging potatoes from the snow.
I am hiding with my baby birds,
who will not keep quiet.

I shall not tell my daughter yet,
put off the moment, can't speak of it
in the trail of her bright innocence.

Some say God no more abandoned them
than the wind abandons a swallow's wing;
that the answer is as close to the question
as breath.

Can you not feel the ethereal dead
tearing at the veil till it's almost rent?

And what if I told you all those bones and teeth
hold for me a terrible beauty?

Anne Frank's Sister Falls from Her Bunk
Bergen-Belsen, 1945

From the well of my bunk
I watch you fall. You do not stir
when I call or scratch at the lice that infect us all.
The cold-booted guard gives you a little kick.
A dirge plays on my frozen lips.
Water and dark earth, to which we return;
that's what you sound like, dragged from the room.

Three days pass without you here.
The typhus unfurls its crimson flowers.
I try to speak but find I have no mouth.
I'm a black dog, muzzled.
To say 'heart' is unheard of.

Each night I climb a few more rungs
up the ladder out of myself
into the attic where we hid once, quiet as bones.
The sky is improbably blue.
I am rising like smoke towards you.

Old Nazis
Diamond Creek, Melbourne

On a forked path by the creek we meet.
They have cataracts and crusty skin.
Their gums recede.
He walks with a discernible limp;
she with the assistance of a stick.
I know them but they don't know me,
this Nazi couple whose guileless talk
eddies like a branch that's caught
between rocks in shallow water.
The Jew in me rises an equivocal fist
beneath this stand of poplar trees,
whose silver leaves murmur each to each.
They are two old Nazis after all
who've long lost interest in their cause,
the urge to search attics or under floors.
My dog tugs on its leash as if to say:
'Well then, we'd best be moving on,'
catching the scent of fox and rabbit.
So civilly we offer our salutations.
The dog and I resume our pace
as the couple dither and vacillate,
debating which path is best to take,
like any elderly folk on this wintry day.

Why Old People Talk about Their Operations

Because the body is vocal as it nears the end
with its querulous list of aches and pains
that makes relatives squeamish.

But the body doesn't care.
Everything grumbles and complains.
The ground has become perilous.

Because our bowels are slow, the bladder stings
and the body is a mulish obstinate thing
whose hipbones jut out beneath flaps of skin.

Our log-jammed senses no longer grasp
the complexity of things; keen, subtle-edged.
Birdsong is a smudge on soft-torn wings.

Because sentences meander and lose their way
though we circle well-trod, familial terrain.
Visitors get restless – we forget their names.

And the heart anticipates that vital day
when it can at last take rest and refrain
from its incessant loyal pumping.

Because the roof has long begun to leak,
the pointing crumbles soon as it's fixed
and nothing else prevails but this.

The Concept of Necessity in Marx and Angels
i.m. Wallis Suchting, philosopher (1931–1997)

'Who, if I cried out, would hear me among the angelic orders?'
— Rainer Maria Rilke, *Duino Elegies: The First Elegy*

Who, if he had cried out, would have heard him?
Only the wind retrieving pages from his hand,
mathematical formulae whizzing in the margins
as he slipped quietly from that conundrum,
no longer burdened by breath or heartbeat.
The smell of sugarcane from the early years
drifting up through furrows between tall green stalks,
and the buttons on his father's police suit hovering.
Back towards birth, where they say his damp hair
was a question-marked whorl at the nape of his neck.

Leaves fall brightly, but the philosopher is gone.
Once, on this day, Copernicus was born.
Outside their separate windows, distanced by centuries,
the starlight's imperative with curiosity.
Night treads the trees, but he is already
eddying towards the hard place
that is God and all unanswered questions,
sinking down the amniotic layers
beyond civilisation and its discontents.
No angels here save Engels, rustling sensible wings;
closer now the face of Marx, and Dante
in the darkening wood, who waits at every turn.

Why are we not quiet as birds in the wake of disaster,
or still like fish beneath ice?
For this was a man who loved not only learning
but those to whom he imparted it,
preparing his classes like full-bodied wines,
reading the bible in hieroglyphic Greek
though God for him was no more than one blind eye
inclined slightly away from the irreverent horizon.

Do you want to hear more?
About Hegel with whom he grappled in German
despite everything?
The poor translation which dropped misery like small stones
into the pit of his intelligence?
Conferences that stole him from his library
and what is more constant: the slow move of knowledge,
as if up through earth. Books grown fibrous with reading,
complex ideas hidden like shapes within wood
that he whittled away at, bit by bit,
while the autumn light slanted into his room,
along generous shelves, down the leg of a desk
to where his paper on logic had fallen,
and where they found him.

Thylacine

Pouched dog pacing back and forth,
if we could bring you back we would
and recreate each tiger stripe,
each vertebra, that tight-hinged jaw.

The early photographers believed
our retinae caught what we last saw.
What might haunt *you*, thylacine,
if science resurrected your corpse?

Frozen concrete, iron bars,
meat gone rancid, shit on the floor.
Four million years in an untamed world
meant freedom could only be bought
by death, the cage door swung open
to the place where dead things go.

Tasmanian tiger, zebra-wolf,
how might you be summoned
now your memory's thin and rare?
Just a few quiet bones and photographs,
this embryo in its formaldehyde jar.

And what else might we seek to restore,
long extinguished, that we now mourn?

Calling Up the Dead

(i)
All roads return her to the burnt-out block,
her throat thick and hoarse with shouting.

Nothing appears. Only this flinty silence,
calcified like chalk, the failing light.

Her calls rebound the hills, return empty.
No cat appears to wind about her legs.

'I planned to marry here,' she says, scratching
a charcoal tree's black trunk, hoping to find

a trace of green. But there was none that day.
When spring unfurls a few unruly shoots

she curls up in the darkening grass until
the father of her children finds her there,

shrouded by rain. But no one, not even he,
can tap the depth or breadth of her sadness.

(ii)
When thunder shakes the mountain
he retreats inside the safe house

of his mother's skirts, her bready scent.
Wind-catchers spinning in the yard

dispute the storm's malevolence.
But he's not convinced.

Squalls like these always return him
to the day the sky turned black,

his teenage uncle cursing roads
he couldn't see for smoke and ash.

The birds that fell from trees,
the stumbling, panicked beasts

all mouthed one word, *mother*, to him
before the fire's jet roar took everything.

(iii)
The sun is low and caught upon the trees
when she recalls the horse, its death a prompt

for other griefs; her children's innocence
lost to them now, like water in a sieve.

At times like these she takes the plaited tail
out from the hidden paddock of a drawer,

inhales the quintessential scent of horse
and hay; nostalgic, opulent and coarse.

Her son, too young to know how rituals work
to ease the past's plurality, takes hold

and thwacks the tail against the kitchen wall
as if at flies, till she retrieves the thing.

A year has passed and still she wakes to find
the house is full of smoke, the horses gone.

Some Adjustments to the Original Idea

Now all the churches have been sold
and countless cataclysms dissolved
the thought that god, if god exists,
could feed the poor, vanquish disease,
placate the sea, obliterate war,
>   or intervene in anything.

And all those plagues and frogs
are folktales, faint-recalled.
The monastery doors clanged shut,
the priests retrained or plain forgot
and nuns just some quaint memory
of distant aunts who dangle
from the family tree; dry
seedless fruit that no one cares
to pick
>   or eat.

Still god's couriers keep beating
at the glassy surface of our dreams.
A jar rolls through the soul's white sleep,
the wind's hand settles a winter field
and bits of god
>   get caught
in the rolling, animal rhythm of things;
the palette of a night-moth's wing,
the motes that slant
>   through forest leaves.

– 3 –

All Things

Persephone
How can I tell her, my own mother,
that I long for the autumn to turn?
When first I take his seeds upon my tongue
I gag, but soon I swallow them with ease.
The earth swallows me in turn.
The bright world fades, means nothing.
I give it scant thought.

Demeter
I am your mother.
What else can I do but wait?
I gnaw at the barren plum trees
until my gums are bleeding,
but nothing hastens your return
or the first pale fruits of spring.
I have waited out more winter days
than I care to count.
I wring my hands until the bones grate,
and only death to all things will quell
my nerves. Darkness may relinquish you
for a season or two, but it is not enough,
is never enough.

Night Feeding
Mitcham Hospital, Melbourne

No man treads here.
We are the night feeders,
propped up in our silky gowns
bought specially for the journey;
our milk the currency of gold,
our breasts bewitched by the moon.

The midwife cups mine in a practised hand
and draws it to my baby's lips
but still she will not drink.

Wailing rises in the room like a hymn,
nurses glide luminously about,
tears fall from me in veils
but the night feeders remain silent.
Suckling destroys all talk.

In the lounge my husband frets.
He wants to be back in the world,
home to dog and dinner, a smoke out the back.
But I am miles away behind the curtain.
Each time he tries to approach,
we repel him with our incantations.

The Virgin Mary Gets Postnatal Depression

I loved being pregnant.
True, I was troubled when Gabriel appeared.
My stomach turned at the smell of sheep,
harsh words had me crying,
but then things settled.
Neighbours gave me tall jars of milk;
every day the doorstep crammed,
the path shrouded in palm leaves
and it was 'Praise be to God' wherever I went.
I felt blessed as the city of heaven,
touched by God's own hand,
which was very reassuring.

Soon I felt him turn and shift,
my faith quickening to consider it.
My flesh filled out his carapace of skin
and my heart pumped tributaries of blood
into the ocean where he twirled;
small bird-frog, breath-like thing.

Joseph wasn't all that thrilled.
'If it's not my child,' he said, 'then whose?'
It was his idea to go to Bethlehem
on the back of that wall-eyed donkey.
Of course there was no room at the inn.
The cattle loosed their bowels,
the chickens ascended in balls of panic.

Neither Matthew nor Luke note the minutiae:
the stench of beasts kept inside too long,

the star's dogged light.
My hips cradled the baby's cruel weight.
His skull rammed my softness.
When it was over, I was exultant
as the angels, clarion-clear.
Son? What a strange, new taste that word had!
I examined the starfish cluster of his fingers.
'It's little Aedon!' I said, which means *Lord* and *fiery*.
'Actually,' said Gabriel, 'It's Jesus Christ.'
So that was that.

I was so hungry I could have eaten an ox
but everyone wanted to see the baby:
thousands of angels hovering like flies,
shepherds standing in the hay,
then those three kings, way past midnight.
My mouth ached from smiling.
While Jesus slept I boiled the rags,
swept the floor, baked the bread, fed the chickens.

Gentle Jesus meek and mild:
how could the psalmists ever know?
When he cried, it was like the whole world crying.
With each new night, my fear rolled in.
I'd wake to think he was in bed with me
and that I'd squashed his terrible softness.
Joseph snored like a camel. If he woke,
he'd swear and turn his back on me.
Around my heart a dark fog settled.
I called for my mother but she didn't hear.

I called for my father; he was in the prayer-house.
I summoned the angels, who did their best.
'Do not be afraid,' they said. 'God is with you.'
But somehow I didn't believe it,
my faith slipping like a horse's shoe and no one to tell:
not Elizabeth busy with baby John, not God.

Old Baba, when she visited, placed her hands
on Jesus' chest to check that he was breathing
and worried the goat would eat him.
'I saw it in the yard,' she said. 'Eating the washing!'
'My baby is the Son of God,' I said.
'He is watched over, protected,' and so on,
but knowledge would not placate her.
Joseph's mother was a practical woman
but he sent her away.
Joseph was a man who liked his space.

Three months passed like this,
climbing uphill as if through sand.
Sometimes I dreamt that God gave up on me,
that the angels departed in flocks of gold.
Then one morning something flew in.
I lifted the child out of his cradle
and as I held him to my breast
he smiled at me.

Rung by rung, out of the well I climbed,
the darkness slowly rolling from me.
A fierce love flared up between us.

Ellipsis
i.m. Jacques Piccard (1922–2008)

Five years it's been since Piccard woke
to find his wife would not

and still the bed is polar cold,
his dreams snow blind.

Most nights he sleeps beside the stove,
his feet fire-warm, descending

to the world that has no sun,
his bathyscaphe groaning a symphony

until its touchdown on the deep-sea bed
where crabs fidget on the ellipsis of memory.

And there he stays, as if in another galaxy,
amongst constellations of dim-lit fish

until morning hauls him up too soon
back to his room where the fire's gone cold,

incredulous as always that the clock's gold hands
measure something as intangible as time,

which extends in all directions,
especially the past.

Amphibian

This shifting, aqueous country of sea
we enter when dreaming or just asleep
distorts the dying, light-crammed stars
and our long discarded, unkempt pasts,
traverses continents and latitudes of memory;
phosphorous, amphibian, primeval.
The sea, when questioned, says:
'Look, the turtles are dancing!
See how the waves resuscitate shells?'
In the dream that's the sea,
I'm nine months deep with full rounded belly;
heartbeat, moon skull, dactyl, etcetera.
In the broken cities, big fish skulk
and the airless ones drift in the drowning skies,
pointing upwards to heaven or the surface.
These things I take down with me:
bright light and breathing fluid
that our bodies remember
    our bodies remember.

Tall Ships

About the future, the mountains were silent,
at least in this country, where everything
inclines towards the past. The wind, the rain;
they never spoke of it. The fire never sang
of unimagined cities tethered to its shores.
If we had heard of boats with wings,
well, that was one of many stories;
and if we dreamt of magic vessels
flickering on the world's blue rim,
that was one of many dreams.

Strange men from afar,
how you glided inexorably towards us
across the sea's dark skin,
pale as the ghosts of our ancestors.
(How long had we awaited *them*!)
I was young; my head a shell
that thoughts like small soft creatures
occupied, and secret things not yet desired.
But when the tall ships sailed into our bay,
I knew that they had come to stay.

Silver City
Broken Hill, New South Wales

Down the invisible coils of thought you go,
down rungs of darkness, to where your father's ghost
still wanders long-armed tunnels, mute and silver
veined, his shift twelve hours too long.

Always you see him like this, his face upturned
until the candle sinks into itself and he's nothing
substantial. Memory stumbling; moist, furred
and horse-blind down these subterranean roads.

'Don't be a miner, son,' he'd say,
not really meaning it. Knowing too well
how fortune landslides, the mind
trailing away like a thin yellow dog

and not much good to anyone.
But that first day he showed you how to split
the rock's hard flank until it sang like silver!
Remember the smell of silver?

Now the mine leans on its elbow
and broods over the town, the streets
named after metal. So you're always
one mile under and descending fast

through windows thick with lead dust
and the past; the knock-off bell going hell
for leather, your father's hands brimful
with rocks from the dark place below.

The God You Don't Believe In

To think that it has come to this,
having dispensed so many degrees
alongside gowned and wizened peers

with whom you used to gather
in this same university café
where we now meet.

Their rush of wet-eared intellect
once left you exuberant and inflamed;
ideas roped into language

that you swung on without effort,
as if over a river from bank to bank
all the way home.

You never had need of a god before,
nor should you now – except
your father's dead, fresh-buried,

and there's no conduit between sky and earth
down which your grief might travel;
he was the one you could call upon.

Has he really been plucked from this little earth
so unceremoniously, like a plant
over whose absence the soil closes?

'God is a fairy tale,' your father said,
and you put your faith in this.
'God is a crutch for the weak,'

spearing the asparagus on his plate.
'If God exists, he's a bastard,' he said,
summoning up all those Jews

gassed and incinerated, tossed into pits
or left to die where they fell in the snow.
Is there a god anywhere even capable of this?

When I ask how you are feeling
about your father's death, you only say
he has appeared to you in dreams.

Nothing more. Just this silence, empty
of content, as we sit sharing a meal
but not much else, except perhaps

the unravelling of your quietude
that has you clutching at a chair
and the god you don't believe in,

for whom there is no provision,
no place at the table of your sorrow.
Just this singular old man with a beard

pointing his lightning-bolt finger;
a kindergarten god, unfed and stunted.
No wonder you have no faith in him

when longing resides elsewhere,
though you can't quite put a name to it.
And none of this makes you weird

or less intelligent than your friends,
just a little outside the ways of the world,
which not only gravity turns.

Those for Whom the Metaphors Are Invented

My father talks in metaphors,
sweeping his hand over the tablecloth
like a cloud above the desert
where this café squats uneasily.
The salt shaker's a light plane flying
round a sugar bowl mountain,
one of many submerged perils.
He speaks of fogs and thunderstorms,
of flying into them and how to get out
with both engines intact.
And he'll do anything to get there,
flying in his paper plane through a river of night.
He's the ice-man, straw-man, cardboard-packer, coal-shoveller,
and there's a son in this for whom the metaphors are invented,
already in the distance and slipping away
into the sea where broken crates bob,
and pigeons, while my father's ship steers on
towards the shining place that seems to promise
land, land, land.

In My Mother's Kitchen

There were no rules
in my mother's kitchen.

My cupcakes had black icing,
her toffee apples were blue.

We melted wax for candles:
a yellow owl I kept for years.

It was peaceful at the bench,
blue-veined like winter skin.

My mother's bones are thin
and light as bird bones now.

She forgets to make the tea.
Lately she's been shedding

all the things she doesn't need.
I salvage her longhand recipes.

'When you are gone,' I say,
'I shall remember everything.'

Orbit

How much does the heart weigh?
Can loss be held like water, or stone?
How long did it take to build the floor of heaven?
Where is the country of forgiveness?
How may I trace its uneasy orbit?
For whom does the blue train whistle?

Exodus

The moon's drifting away from us
in small but steady increments.
Its gradual exodus suggests
one day we'll see no more of it
than a tiny orb that scarce lights up
its limits.

Beneath the dark and moonless nights
women's menses will start to wane
in rhythm with the sluggish tides.
The old and frail will cease to feel
that lunar pressure on their heels.

Back in those god-crowded, druidic days
the moon was close, a white gold god
whose pitted face young children climbed.
Now only a few incline their gaze,
scanning the sky's dark carapace.

Moon dust is a faint irritant
our bones contain.

Walking the Black Dog

1.
Large black dog who invades my room
in the margin between sleep and wake
to dig my grave with your paws.
Five seconds is all it takes
for you to cast your dog-shaped
shadow across my sheets.
Even the simple act of swinging
my legs out of bed becomes impossible.
Outside the morning lengthens
into a season that won't change.
The corella sounds its wake-up call,
but anything I'd planned to do today
you've tipped out of your bowl
until there's only you, black dog,
standing over me.
I dare not move or look away,
lest the ice chill of your breath
freeze me over completely.

2.
So you're here again.
I thought that you had slunk
back into the black of your own shadow.
But mark how slyly you've returned,
larger than ever and more forlorn,
prowling the void in my abdomen.
Never did I suspect my interior
to hold such swamps and flatlands;

brackish, drab and monotone
from shore to distant shore.
Traversing any distance is difficult
when you sit silent at my core
and conjure up armchairs,
into which I fall.

3.
Did we meet when you were young
and soft-bellied? Did I let you in my door
one wintry day, with the best intentions,
not knowing how unwieldy you would grow?
I'm not in the habit of discarding pets,
but even if I did, you'd refuse to go.
You are most present on ordinary days;
in the dull bulk of the afternoon
or in the early hours of morning
when your flat, grey voice intones:
'Don't even bother getting out of bed.
There's nothing for you out there today.'

4.
Of course I could try to befriend you
the way I did my own labrador.
But she is golden-warm and solid,
and you're a dog-shaped mist.
If I try to scratch your ears,
my fingers pass right through.

You have no eyes, no tongue, no heart.
No one can see you but me,
and even I less see than sense you tracking me,
not knowing when you'll next appear
to slip beneath my skin,
nonchalant as a dog who marks a tree
by pissing on the trace of things.

5.
I might try to train you, I suppose.
I might say 'no', circle you tightly,
and perhaps you would learn in time
not to break the furniture of my heart.
I might subordinate you, become top of the pack,
ensure I pass through doorways first,
refuse you the luxury of higher ground
like the bed or the couch,
for which you have a preference.
But then we have the problem of your transparency
and formlessness, the ungraspable fog of you,
the shroud of your coldness, settling in.

6.
When I suggest a walk, you slowly
wag your tail. But where can we walk?
Not by the river; you might hurl me in.
Not in the mountains; you might hurl me off.

How deep might you lead me
down paths only trodden in sleep,
into forests of forgetfulness
and dank, discarded dreams?
Will the leaves turn grey beneath your paws?
Today you seem more dog than not,
now that you've uncurled yourself
from the lining of my heart
to stand instead beside me
with a quizzical, half-cocked head,
snuffling at the scent of my retreat.
'Later,' I say, and scratch your neck.
'Soon. That's a good dog. Not yet, not yet.'

Vanishing Point

How we worked at our flying machines,
at the first small strokes of their paper wings;

fanciful, antediluvian things tethered
from the ceilings of solemn museums.

Now flight's a routine, prosaic event,
though the gods still clamour in our ears

and have us muttering scant-used prayers
lest we crash back down to earth or sea.

A quarrel persists (which would be worse?)
as the flight steward smiles robotically

and demonstrates the emergency gear.
Meanwhile, above the tarmac, birds

shift formation with simplicity and ease,
tend to the weft and warp of unseen tapestries,

then dip and wheel at vanishing point
into skies higher than these.

– 4 –

The Way We Do In Sex

Ask me when my tugging oil-slick fist
has you tumescent and butting at my lips;
when every nerve's erect as spinifex
and our skins fluoresce like sand at dawn
on the kind of beach you find up north —
but I digress
        the way we do in sex
where the metaphors overlap and mix.
Ask me while we're freshly peeled
and your sticky death seeds hold me in their thrall.
Ask me, damn it, as you swing the rough spade
of your hardness into soil until it brings me
to my knees —
Just ask, and I'll do whatever it is
        knowing even how this will end.

Triage

I've never been jealous of all those pretty girls
but this one rattles my bones and filters all I see;
even this waning moon
        where she now sits on the pointy tip.
That scarlet pony tail, which nods and dips,
scarce hides her intentions
        — at least not from me.
I can't compete with youth or classical dexterity,
her open palm pressed on your chest.
Those legs wrapped around her cello warn me in dreams
of the fragility of things; bird nests, worn string.
That what's bound fast can be snapped or unravelled
        in an instant, really.

Morning Ride
Eltham Station, 8.01am

School girls whinny and toss their yellow manes
in half-wild herds on board the morning train.

I'll never be like that again. What's quick
in them now slows in me, though I recall

their visceral scent, new-glistening, which makes
grown men and school boys shift, ambivalent

in their vinyl seats. The girls gossip and stamp
their black-laced feet. Some part their legs a bit.

Something's begun, some urgent heartstrong need
for root and seed that no old god can halt,

no worn-out creed. The train groans to a stop.
The girls get off in a flecked-skirt, skittish mob,

disperse. And yet, the taut wire of their want
persists; their sharp desire, its imperative.

Who Is To Say

That Parisian woman who did not like
her children is long gone while I remain,
who love my own too much. Although

her red armchair still occupies the space
beneath the window in your study.
There was the day we tried to move it

but the chair refused to go, wedging
its bulk against the door frame.
Some things are not so easily disposed of

and besides, I like that chair; the way
it holds me when I sit in it to read.
Who is to say what makes someone leave

and brings another in her place?
Only that all past lovers leave
their sultry trace.

Farm girl, you call me, despite mid-age,
working in the garden or fetching mail,
still in my pyjamas, past midday.

Holiday Season
Healesville, 2013

Time sits still in the railway yards,
crouched on the tracks that fork
and split with only the crows to cark
in contemplation.

The old year's scarce been shunted out,
the new one cranked up, freshly minted.
Its keen-oiled elbow pistons glint,
the tracks change route with a little click

and the clock breaks time into finicky bits,
making finite what is infinite.
The sky's lit up temporarily
amidst the barbecues and beer,

the caravans and annexed tents
chockfull of other people's kids.
And everyone is at the beach,
or about to go, or has just been.

I sit by the lake in the newborn year,
where frogs revel in reeds and star-caught
water, rejoicing in their own throat-song
whether I'm here, or gone.

Thoughts between Christmas and New Year

(i) Forgetting to buy the nets
Long hard season of youth
with so much going on inside.
You have become a bird grown bold
while I was busy doing other things.

This summer I forgot to buy the nets
to stop the parrots from tearing
at all that unripe fruit;
the garden a riot of pulp by dawn.

You can perforate my care
with one fierce peck of your beak
or circle just beyond my reach.
But that's okay.

I too was once a daughter,
pelting my own mother
with the still-hard berries
of girlhood.

(ii) Material in excess of 2 cubic metres
It's broken, this contraption we called marriage.
No allen key or spanner will ever fix its bolts
    or hinges.
And all those little cogs and wheels
that used to turn with ease
now screech when I wind up the gears.
I dump it on the verge in spring
for the hard waste collection, or recycling,
but it's in excess of 2 cubic metres, apparently.
They only take mattresses and fridges,
    that sort of thing.
Each year I dismantle another piece.
The council takes it, by degrees.

(iii) But then, that said
Now my mother's an octogenarian,
words elude her;
      our talk alighting on this
or that as she sifts through phrases
in her head where sentences hover
just out of reach

      she forgets
what I told her yesterday
or this time last week.
And all my childhood friends
whom she once bathed and fed
                            are gone
now from her head
but our pet dogs, budgies, cats and fish
remain as clear as when we first invented
      names for them

and her face still holds that light
by which we live. But then, that said,
the sun is most luminous
      just before it sets.

Moorings

Somewhere in Switzerland
there's a house where I could have lived.
There are sons and daughters never born.
In the gaps on my shelves, books I never wrote.

At fifteen, I didn't know how pretty I was.

At eighteen, the world was malleable, soaring up
like the soft shell of a cathedral, newly laid, its spire
wavering this way and that.

At fifty, I'm moored to this lichen pier.
My small boats bob on the ocean rim.

'Gone!' cries the house by the blue Swiss lake.
'Gone!' cry the babies and blank-spined books.

Who knows if the ropes that anchor me
will snap or slowly unravel?
Only that I'm drifting towards the sea
that flows surely out of this one.

What to Expect

Those pregnancy books don't hint at this.
They're absorbed by the body's burgeoning,
by what to eat and how to breathe.
But I guess they can't cover everything.

Clamouring child with autumn caught
in your tangled hair, gazing out
from your mother's lair, too big
yet not quite old enough to leave.

The artist has drawn you well, but sketchily;
a slight figure on the road's pencil curve,
just a smudge of charcoal to suggest
your quotidian movement.

Waking from Hibernation

Winter has left me slow, bear-fat;
my pale body folded into sleep.
Spring's right on time
       — but I'm not ready for its urgency;
the buds that burst on lemon trees,
the pigeons cooing subliminally,
my dog coiled tight till I unclip the lead
and she runs in helix trajectories
after spores I can neither track nor sniff.
I lumber towards the fecund ridge
       where a tentative sun wakens me.

First Cigarette
Yarrawonga, 1976

At night the darkness was wool-thick
till dawn shoved its persistent fingers in.
Breakfast was fit for farmers and kings.
Lindy, boy-chested and bony-ribbed,

ate half loaves of bread with quince jelly.
I ate more tentatively.
But everyone was well fed here;
our horses grew as fat as seals

on lucerne paddocks gone to seed.
The diamantine water, the emerald slopes
were infused with a paradisiac purity
as we galloped our horses across the fields,

smoked cigarettes that Lindy filched,
and when they ran out, wheat grass
in the pages of magazines. Lindy's idea;
hooked at twelve on nicotine.

When my father called, I dipped my head,
so his kisses fell on my riding hat
and not my cheeks, for fear he'd smell
my smoky breath.

'What's this?' he said.
But I said nothing.
Eve in the garden, hiding from God,
having picked of the fruit and tasted it.

Dragonfly
Black Saturday, February 2009

A dragonfly hovered by my front door
as if it had lost its way to where dragonflies go
on hot, dry days when the leaves hang limp
      and panting.

Magpies sprawled; wings splayed, gape-beaked.
The galahs wound up their infant's wail
and the cicadas shrilled a song they'd sung
                      all summer.

That jewel-flecked fly caught a squall of wind.
I watched it rise on transparent wings
and hoped it found some cleft of stone and shade
where the water falls white,
like bridal veils
      — before the sky went black
and the firestorm came.

– 5 –

There Are Stones That Sing

'Oh, gleaming generosity, how can they write you out?'
— Mary Oliver

The churches are almost empty or sold,
as if they've reached their tipping point,
and from the pulpits, god slid out.

And all that fanciful gold leaf
on heaven's floor was incinerated
by our telescopes, whose lenses caught
it in their scope. And bits of tattered
god fell down.

I've heard that *âme* ('soul' in French)
is the name of a wooden chip,
very exposed and vulnerable,
that violin makers insert into
the bodies of their instruments
to further enhance the sound.
So maybe that's where god
lives now.

If you ask a priest, he'll point up.
If you ask black fellas, they'll point down
to stones that sing and rivers
vibrating underground.

Shift Work

(i) Case Notes
In a government house six children live
brimful with anger beyond their years,

punched in the womb and kicked in the teeth
before protective services brought them here

away from the city to these yellow hills
that speak to earth, grass, sky and wind.

Driving home at the end of my shift,
trace of urine from wet bed sheets

and something kicking against my ribs,
the way you'd kick at a chair leg, absently.

(ii) Wild Rabbits
A magpie sings outside the window.
It's Saturday, the morning hours

suspended like these couch girls
who watch *Buffy the Vampire Slayer*

repeats, in limbo between sleep and wake.
One girl's belly is curdled, thick as cream,

the other glowers and bares her teeth.
'What the fuck? Stop looking at me.'

I'm not looking at her, actually, but
beyond to where six heifers ruminate

on a hillside lush with grass and a herd
of roos stand still as tree stumps.

Wild rabbits complete this pastoral scene.
But beyond the flat screen's flickering

the two girls can't see anything,
shut firmly as the security door

that keeps some kids out and others in,
and only opens with a master key.

(iii) Talking about Country
Bare-rooted sonnet plucked straight
from the earth, shaking dirt

from her mouth in irregular metre;
she's all anapests and trochees,

arrhythmic, not knowing who her mob
might be or what its dreaming is.

Talk about god, she'll say god doesn't exist,
as abruptly as if she's been hit or kicked.

Talk about country, she'll give you
a blank-eyed stare. She was loved once,

if fleetingly, before terror erased all odds
for feeling. They took her away then,

the tin roof of her home flapping
like a broken wing, grown smaller

and smaller, as the government car
sped her around that final corner.

(iv) Incident Report
In this place, everything absconds,
even the goats, cartoon-comical

with their quizzical beards, bellies
swinging like a hearty laugh.

I volunteer to catch them at it,
knowing this is a better gig

than making sandwiches for kids
who spit in my tea and cut their skin.

The goats are light relief, a cameo
in this tragedy where there is no word

for empathy. Five times they escape
on neat-folded knees beneath the fence

before I twig. The fugitive trotting
of their cloven hooves announces them

in an instant, it seems; their rectangular
eyes see a goat-shaped world that doesn't

include me. When I block the gap, they're
confounded by what will no longer yield.

Tomorrow they'll escape another way,
as all kids do from this sanctuary.

Dutch Tulip Bubble
Amsterdam, 1637

For the bulbs were brought back from Constantinople by a botanist, but neighbours stole them from his garden.

For they were in colours not yet invented, with lurid flesh-whorls that made women blush and men offer up just about anything; their inheritances, suits of clothes, their wives, or beds.

For the bulbs, worth more than gin, herring and cheese, were far too valuable to grow or plant. In an unfortunate incident, a sailor mistook one for an onion and almost ate it for breakfast.

For the mother bulbs could take years to birth, the daughter bulbs more vigorous but not so strong, and the finest specimens infertile as mules; their colours produced by mildew and disease.

For the bulbs passed from fist to fist in the smoky back rooms of taverns, and figures were scrawled on scraps of paper for flowers that were never seen.

For the tulip bubble burst like all others, leaving grown men weeping in the snow on their knees.

Spinning on a Dream Thread

'In the new landscape, there will be only cars.'
— Bruce Dawe

In dream I saw a host of arachnids
that climbed about the universe and cast

silk lines from spinnerets to hold the earth
in filaments so sheer they were concealed

from human eyes. Until I woke and all
vanished, except a corner of this trance

to worry at, a stray thread from the dream
cloth's weft that told me little more of it.

As the governments debated carbon tax
and which highway ought be extended next,

the earth took emphysemic breaths
beneath the weight of cars and bitumen,

cathedrals drowned beneath the rising tides
and the last blue whale up and died.

Though all about me I could keenly sense
celestial spiders casting out new webs

at measured pace that neither slowed nor sped,
regardless of how fast we broke the threads.

Open Plan Office

I'm not accustomed to it; the mandatory
lunch breaks & 8.30am starts,
the cubicles divided by particle board,

the time in lieu & sick leave forms,
the perennial cakes & sandwiches
left over from meetings & morning tea.

I'm in the Bushfire Recovery Unit
where memorials for the dead are not art,
I'm told. My team leader deletes the word

from all my tenders & reports
while the manager's touring Europe,
taking photos of cars in car museums

& the woman from Permits next to me,
critiquing last night's reality TV, says:
'Yep, I know just what you mean.'

Virga, or No Rain Falling

Rain that doesn't hit the ground
but just falls through me in a mist;

slight missives from the otherworld
that dissolve before I can decipher them.

Grasses incline their delicate throats
to catch the minute droplets.

Cattle tear at mouthfuls of green
and leaf-weed, their damp hides

effervescent with this alphabet of mist
too light to be called rain.

Just this most subtle of utterances,
with what's left unsaid glittering, nonetheless.

The Leaf Sweeper
After Wordsworth's 'The Leech-Gatherer'

On one of those fretful, gust-ridden days when the sky
seems fed up with its own mushroom-bellied haze,
I came across a woman for whom the bell tongue
of mortality had long tolled; her dress a faded garden
hung on limbs so gaunt it seemed her very bones
should lie now in some ill-dug grave, or haunt
the house that tumbled down the hill behind her.
Yet stand she did on her front porch, sweeping
leaves from her rambling steps, which dwindled
like a sentence raised, half-thought and discarded again.

Often I had chance to walk right past her house,
as was the habit of my dog to run this way
through weeds in green and tangled skeins,
and each time found her sweeping up the leaves
flung down by a glacial wind that howled
across these hills. Never a thought she seemed
to give the repetition of her task, the foliage
cast-off stitches from the fabric of her trees,
falling and blown away, only to be hoarded
up again by this gnarled and ancient maid.

Until one day I had recourse to ask her why:
my dog, having escaped its lead, took freedom
at a leap and gambolled onto her property.
And as I set about the chore of catching it,
thus done, she gave pause long enough to say:
'Because what falls on stone gives no reprieve,
but earth's revived by leaf shrouds such as these.
Not for myself do I sweep the pathways clean
but for the world; so many corpses, buried soft,
give rise to new growth, no thing lost.'

I resumed my walk, imbued with new intent;
that the dead slept on yet did their work
in the porous soil my feet now trod.
And she resumed her regenerative chores;
a gruff figure receding on that flank of earth,
which breathed out beneath its fertile pelt
and just as quietly in.

War Horse

After *Napoleon Crossing the Alps* **by Jacques-Louis David**

Napoleon was a small man who did big things
many other small men wouldn't dare to do.
But sitting for portraits made him fidgety

so we don't see much of him here.
This painting is all horse and Napoleon
a mere emblem of ideal leadership,

when actually, he rode to this battle by mule,
not the fiery steed he requested here,
rearing high on meaty haunches.

One thing's clear:
if great men die with ceremony,
not so their horses.

Just this bulk smashing into hard earth
and the belly twisting piteously
as the battle continues on.

Another Poem about Dogs

How does anyone do anything?
Some days are more difficult than others.

Evenings are easier, having shucked off
the shadow that tugs at me;
dark sister who slows my awakening.

Sadness is invisible, unlike broken bones.
You can be loved and still the centre
does not hold.

The interior can't be traversed
by ordinary means; an ash-black boat
with tattered sails reaps the depths
for bones and teeth.

Until here we are at the heart of it
where everything is skeletal,
even the dog that howls:
a skeletal dog with a skeletal jaw
that catches the bone I throw for it
as it lopes along the shoreline.

Even the darkest tides recede;
pin pricks of light in a glassy sea,
faint stars guiding me home.

Small Deaths

So many mice we have poisoned
or trapped, while this one ran plump
and sort of free, growing bald

and grey, with shrivelled ears
and geriatric at the age of three,
despite diligence on its exercise wheel.

I dig a small grave beneath a tree.
My daughter marks it with a little rock.
The dog wags its tail unknowingly,

sole pet remaining in our menagerie;
the hole for its body as yet undug,
as it is for all other living things.

The Interior Ladder

'Now that my ladder's gone, I must lie down where all the
ladders start'
— William Butler Yeats

It's like finding a room inside yourself
but the door is so high you can't reach it,
or perhaps you just hadn't noticed it before
until you lose something precious or important
like your job or your health or your marriage
or worse, someone vanishes from your orbit.

And the world you've been polishing so carefully
crashes to the floor so you just can't mend it
or it rolls across the lawn and you can't find it,
though you crawl on hands and knees
in the grass long after nightfall
and the crickets have ended their chorus.

And you keep on looking until the days
turn into months, the months
into the leaf litter of years.
By now you've forgotten about the room
if you ever noticed it at all.
Instead you get busy, traversing oceans
and continents until your ship lists badly
to starboard and your horse is gaunt
and collapsing beneath you.

You try to think if there is anywhere else
you might seek to replace what you have lost,
but you've run out of oceans and continents
and ships and horses. So you return
to the place where it all began,
where you lost what you never found.
And you are hungry for revenge,
bear-angry for all the years lost
on that ship and that horse.
If you could find the thing you lost
you would smash it, you think.
You would smash it into a thousand bits
and stomp it into the ground or burn it
or do whatever it takes to be rid of it.
You want to do to it what it did to you.
So you try that for a while,
but it's like trying to punch a hole in the sky
or tear down the stars. Because it's gone,
this thing, and it's never coming back.

And that's when you remember the room
with the door so high up you can't reach it
or perhaps you see it for the first time.
And even though it's nothing special,
just a room with a door, you're all out
of places to look, so this might as well
be the last.

You go next door to borrow a ladder
from your neighbours, who argue about
who lent it out last and who put it back.
Things start to get nasty.
'Look,' you say. 'Don't worry about it.'
And return to your own house.

But somehow it looks different,
like a house that is both yours and isn't,
like a house in a dream you might
have had and now faintly recall.
Someone has propped a ladder against
its wall, the way they do in dreams.
So you begin to climb.
The room is much higher than you thought
but you keep on climbing, though the days
turn to months, the months to the leaf litter
of years. But finally you reach it.
You are starving and aching. Every bone
in your body is sore. But you have just
enough in you to take hold of the handle.
And you open the door.

A NOTE ON THE TEXT

p. 39 Wallis Arthur Suchting was a philosopher and Associate Professor at Sydney University NSW, remembered for the brilliance of his scholarship and generosity of knowledge. Sadly, Suchting took his own life in 1997.

p. 54 Jacques Piccard was a Swiss oceanographer and engineer, known for developing the bathyscaphe, a deep-sea submersible vehicle. The prototype was invented by his father, Auguste Piccard. In 1960, Jacques Piccard embarked on a voyage to the bottom of the sea in his own bathyscaphe, the *Trieste*. The descent took five hours and reached a record depth of 35,800 feet.

SOURCES FOR THE EPIGRAPHS

Bruce Dawe. 'In the New Landscape.' *Sometimes Gladness: Collected Poems, 1954–2005*. Melbourne: Longman Cheshire, 2006.

Mary Oliver. 'Some Things, Say the Wise Ones.' *Why I Wake Early*. Boston: Beacon Press, 2004.

Rainer Maria Rilke. *The Duino Elegies*. 1931. Trans. Edward Snow Young. New York: North Point Press, 2000.

William Butler Yeats. 'The Circus Animals' Desertion.' 1939. *Selected Poems*. London: Penguin, 2000.

Author's note

South in the World is essentially about the struggle to maintain a balance between those southern and northern poles by which we navigate the world: between ordinary living and the desire to transcend it, between earth and sky, body and spirit, descent and ascent, the real and ethereal, the mundane and exotic.

In part, the dynamic of this book is incarnational. It wants to bring vitality from the ethereal realm into the everyday: to construct a universe out of airy thinness and, at the same time, remain connected to the earth's solidity. The poetry moves from a higher, loftier stance to a more communal, domestic one, towards what D. H. Lawrence refers to as 'social compact': the impulse for human connection.

God in his faded cardigan, the Virgin Mary, Anne Frank, Jacques Piccard, Napoleon, winged horses and angels variously intersect in this book with ageing parents, daughters, lovers, ex-husbands, shift work, damaged adolescents, and family pets.

The bushfire poems indicate an entrance into a wider sphere concerned with suffering and catastrophe: Black Saturday 2009, the attempted genocide of the Jews, and the less spectacular destruction of the self through ageing and dereliction. Yet in the midst of this new landscape blighted by cataclysm, there are moments of greening and redemption.

Several poems take the theme of mothers and fathers, perhaps because the descent into the incarnate world of matter requires us to deal with domesticity and familial relationships. As Patrick White has said, mothers and fathers are the price we pay to enter life – a life that also binds us to day jobs, bureaucracy and open plan offices.

Poets, to my mind, are guardians of myth and imagination. They keep enchantment alive in a prosaic century, invoke the invisible, and nudge us towards the one thing that can redeem our human lot: strengthening our connections with mystery and the eternal.

Many poems in this collection have been previously published or broadcast. My gratitude to editors and producers of the following: *ABC Poetica, The Age, The Medical Journal of Australia, The Bruce Dawe National Poetry Prize, Australian Love Poems 2013, Award Winning Australian Writing 2012, The Best Australian Poems 2010, Cordite Poetry Review, The Global Poetry Anthology 2013, Heat, The Newcastle Poetry Prize Anthology 2000, Psychoanalytic Perspectives, Scintillae, Space: New Writing, The Stars Like Sand: Australian Speculative Poetry* and *Kinglake 350* by Adrian Hyland, who selected the poem, 'Girls and Horses in the Fire', as the epigraph for his book on the Victorian bushfires.

Many friends and colleagues have in various ways contributed to the development of these poems. My heartfelt thanks to you all. In addition, I want to thank those organisations and people who have been especially significant in the production of this book:

The Literature Board of the Australia Council for the Arts, for awarding me the 2012 New Works Grant that made it possible to complete the manuscript.

My readers, Chris Wallace-Crabbe and Alex Skovron, for their time on the manuscript and careful, astute suggestions.

The efficient team at UWA Publishing and my editor Terri-ann White, who steered at the helm with such dexterity and good humour.

David Tacey and Hayley Austen, who know too well what it is to live with a poet in the house.

www.ingramcontent.com/pod-product-compliance
Lightning Source LLC
Chambersburg PA
CBHW032055150426
43194CB00006B/530